D1032206

17157

DEMCO

CROWN MATRIMONIAL

Crown
Matrimonial

A FULL-LENGTH PLAY
by ROYCE RYTON

NELSON DOUBLEDAY, Inc.
Garden City, New York

This play was first presented by Michael Codron at the Haymarket Theatre, London, October 19, 1972. The cast was as follows:

Queen Mary	Wendy Hiller
Page to Queen Mary	Leonard Cracknell
Mabell, Countess of Airlie	Joan Haythorne
The Hon. Margaret Wyndham	Barbara Atkinson
King Edward VIII (David)	Peter Barkworth
The Princess Royal (Mary)	Jane Wenham
The Duchess of Gloucester (Alice)	Heather Kyd
Mr. Monckton, K.C.	Noel Johnson
The Duke of York (Bertie)	Andrew Ray
The Duchess of York (Elizabeth)	Amanda Reiss

CROWN MATRIMONIAL had its American premiere at the Helen Hayes Theatre, New York, October 2, 1973, with the following cast:

Queen Mary	Eileen Herlie
Page to Queen Mary	Richard Sterne
Mabell, Countess of Airlie	Eleanor Phelps
The Hon. Margaret Wyndham	Enid Rodgers
King Edward VIII (David)	George Grizzard
The Princess Royal (Mary)	Paddy Croft
The Duchess of Gloucester (Alice)	Elizabeth Swain
The Duke of York (Bertie)	Patrick Horgan
The Duchess of York (Elizabeth)	Ruth Hunt

The character of Mr. Monckton, K.C., who appears in Act II, Scene 1, was omitted from the Broadway production.

Produced by Lester Osterman, Michael Codron & Richard Horner

Directed by Peter Dews

Scenery & Costumes by Finlay James

Lighting by Neil Peter Jampolis

Synopsis of Scenes

ACT ONE

Scene 1: Late morning in early September 1936
Scene 2: Before dinner, two months later
Scene 3: After dinner, the same evening

ACT TWO

Scene 1: Late morning in early December 1936
Scene 2: Late evening, two days later
Scene 3: Early evening, two days later
Scene 4: Afternoon nine years later in 1945

The action takes place in Queen Mary's private sitting room on the second floor of Marlborough House, London.

PROLOGUE

AS THE HOUSELIGHTS GO DOWN the Proclamation is heard over the front of house speakers:

Whereas it hath pleased Almighty God to call to His mercy our late Sovereign Lord King George V of blessed and glorious memory, that the High and Mighty Prince Edward Albert Christian George Andrew Patrick David (guns boom) is now, by the death of our late Sovereign of happy memory, become our only (guns) lawful and rightful Liege Lord Edward VIII (guns) by the grace of God; of Great Britain, Ireland, and the British Dominions beyond the seas (guns), King, Defender of the Faith, Emperor of India. God Save the King.

THE CURTAIN RISES

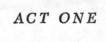

ACT ONE

SCENE ONE

SCENE: *The Queen's drawing-room is on the second floor. Since it is her private drawing-room it reflects her own taste absolutely. This is good. She has a tendency for having only bibelots which are in some way connected with the family. There are big doors up center, a second door right, a big window left, a sofa left, armchairs down right and down left, a desk and chair up left, and a table against the wall down right. At right center is the Queen's armchair, with a small table right of it.*

It is late morning in early September 1936.

AT RISE OF CURTAIN: LADY AIRLIE (MABELL), *a lifelong friend and lady-in-waiting, is found on stage. She is elderly, dignified and sensible, dressed in traveling clothes. The* PAGE *opens the door up center and the* QUEEN *comes in.* MABELL *rises and curtsies.*

QUEEN

Mabell, dear. How good of you to come here so quickly. (MABELL *and* QUEEN *kiss.*)

MABELL

Your Majesty.

QUEEN

I'm afraid we have very little time. The King has proposed himself for luncheon. I see him so rarely nowadays that I jumped at the opportunity.

MABELL

Quite.

QUEEN

Do sit down, dear. (*The* QUEEN *sits, and so does* MABELL.) You must be exhausted after your journey. Did you have a good crossing?

MABELL

The weather was glorious. It was a mercy when we got out to sea. New York was like an oven. My son very kindly met me at Waterloo. He tells me you've seen Baldwin.

QUEEN

I never stop seeing him.

MABELL

Ma'am, dear, have you spoken to the King yourself?

QUEEN

No, no. Yes, I know I should, but I can't. You have no

conception how extraordinarily difficult and evasive he can be. He's like Queen Alexandra when he wants to be. Charming, vague, elusive. I never have been able to talk to him. Dear Mabell, we can't put off the dreadful moment any longer. Is the American press as bad as they say?

MABELL

Oh, it's worse. She is being openly spoken of as the next queen. One paper has even given the actual date of when she will take up residence in Buckingham Palace.

QUEEN

Are they mad?

MABELL

Far from it. Another paper says that she is being consulted on the redecoration of both Buckingham Palace and Windsor Castle. According to them she's already done over Sandringham and Balmoral. One headline in a Chicago paper referred to her as "Queen Wally."

QUEEN

Wally?

MABELL

W-A-L-L-Y. Her Christian name is Wallis. (QUEEN MARY *braces herself. The shock to her should not be underestimated. Throughout her life the Throne and its occupants have been objects of respect. To have a king, and*

5

that king her son, the object not of respect but of cheap newspaper gossip, disturbs her tremendously. LADY AIR-LIE *is aware of this. She rises and crosses to the window.*) Then this cruise in the Balkans. They have been photographed everywhere together, ma'am. "The King rhumbas with Queen Wally."

QUEEN

Rhumbas?

MABELL

It's a dance. He's been photographed swimming with her, rowing a boat with her, shopping. The King seems to be almost deliberately drawing attention to her. There are endless stories of her family background, her past life, her husbands.

QUEEN

Dear God!

MABELL

Her first husband, who's still alive, was given to drink, I think. As far as I can gather, her own upbringing was actually perfectly respectable, but all the American press are convinced of one thing. The King, they say, intends to marry her.

QUEEN

But there can be no question of marriage. Apart from

6

every other consideration, she's still the wife of Mr. Simpson.

MABELL

She's divorced one husband. Why not a second? (QUEEN MARY *rises in her agitation and moves about.*)

QUEEN

He's—he's head of the Church, Defender of the Faith. It's out of the question.

MABELL

The American press is convinced there's going to be a divorce. Mr. Simpson now resides permanently at the Guards' Club. My son confirms this. Furthermore, the Americans believe the divorce will go through and be made absolute even before the coronation.

QUEEN

What?

MABELL

My solicitor says it's perfectly possible, provided the case is undefended. It's September now; if the case is heard in October she will be free in April. The coronation is still planned for May.

QUEEN

It's nonsense. Sheer nonsense! It must be nonsense. Mustn't it?

MABELL

Everything points to it's not being. The King was received in Istanbul by Ataturk. Mrs. Simpson was beside him the entire time. In an official drive through the streets they sat side by side, for all the world as if they were man and wife. Her friends in London already treat her as if she were queen. They do everything but curtsy to her. Ma'am, so far you have seen the crisis as one of the King being—how shall I put it?—possibly having an open liaison with a married woman. I believe we are going to have a much graver problem than that to face. (*There is a pause. The* QUEEN, *after her instinctive reaction of amazed disbelief, is now in perfect control of herself.*)

QUEEN

It'll be the end of monarchy. I feel ill with shame. There's nothing to stop him, you know, Mabell. The Royal Marriages Act applies to a monarch's relations, not to the monarch himself. He is restrained only by the Law of the Protestant Succession and of course she's not Roman Catholic.

MABELL

No. I'm afraid not.

(MARGARET WYNDHAM, *another lady-in-waiting, comes in. She is devoted to the* QUEEN *but is not on the same intimate terms as* LADY AIRLIE.)

Act One

MARGARET

Do forgive me, ma'am, but the King's car has just driven into the courtyard.

QUEEN

Thank you, Margaret. Mabell, dear, I cannot thank you enough. I wish I could ask you to stay to lunch.

MARGARET

I've arranged for Lady Airlie to have lunch with me, ma'am.

MABELL

That's very kind of you, but I'm meeting Bruce. Will I see you, ma'am, before I go to Scotland?

QUEEN

Oh, I hope so, dear. And if not, the moment you return. Evelyn is making out a fresh rota for my dear ladies, so you will be hearing from her soon.

(PAGE *enters up center.*)

PAGE

His Majesty.

(DAVID [*King Edward VIII*] *comes in. He is forty-two and has been King for only a few months. He is small, with devastating charm and devastating youthfulness.*

9

He looks twenty-five to thirty at the most. He has proved a superbly successful Prince of Wales. The youthful charm is well to the fore. His smile is dazzling.)

DAVID

Mamma. (*All three women curtsy, and he kisses the* QUEEN's *hand.* PAGE *withdraws.*) Please, Mamma. Lady Airlie. Miss Wyndham. (LADY AIRLIE *and* MISS WYNDHAM *murmur "Your Majesty."*)

QUEEN

David, my dear, you look so brown.

DAVID

Well, it was very hot in the Mediterranean. I sunbathed a great deal.

QUEEN

So I gathered. Lady Airlie is just back from America.

DAVID

Really. (*He is quite at his ease. The reference to America leaves him quite unperturbed.*) I'm dying to go there again. I hope to make one of my first state visits to Washington. Do sit down, Lady Airlie.

MABELL

I was just about to go, sir, when you came in.

DAVID

What a shame! I hoped you were staying to lunch.

QUEEN

She's lunching with Bruce.

DAVID

I'm sure my mother would be delighted to see him, too.

MABELL

It's very kind of Your Majesty, but we're having quite a family luncheon. The Queen can hardly be expected to feed the entire Ogilvie clan at a moment's notice.

QUEEN

You are quite a tribe. (*They laugh.*)

DAVID

Give Bruce my love. If he's in Scotland next week, tell him to ring me up at Balmoral. Where were you in America?

MABELL

New York, mostly.

DAVID

Ah, yes. Have you ever been to America, Miss Wyndham?

MARGARET

No, sir.

DAVID

You should go. You'd like it.

MARGARET

Do you think so?

DAVID

I'm sure of it. It's such a wonderful country. Vital and full of pep. (*Laughs.*)

MARGARET

Too full of pep, if the films are anything to go by. I'm sure I should be completely bewildered the entire time. I'm not modern like you, sir. (DAVID, *if aware of an underlying criticism, shows no sign of it.*)

DAVID

Well, we need progress. We must move with the times.

MARGARET

Only if the times are moving in the right direction. I often wonder if they are.

QUEEN

Mabell, dear, we mustn't keep you from your family gathering.

MABELL

Ma'am. Sir. (*She curtsies twice, as does* MARGARET, *and they both withdraw, up center.*)

DAVID

Well . . .

QUEEN

Help yourself, dear. George and Marina tell me you've acquired a taste for the cocktail. But in this house you'll have to make do with a glass of sherry.

DAVID

A glass of sherry will be delicious. (*He smiles at her.*) But cocktails aren't terrible at all. If you could only bring yourself to take the plunge, I'm sure you'd like them.

QUEEN

They have such peculiar names. A Side Lady—a White Car.

DAVID

It's the other way round. It's a Sidecar and a White Lady. (*They laugh. There is something just a little forced about this exchange of pleasantries.*)

QUEEN

Tell me all your news. (DAVID *is pouring out his glass of sherry. He waves the bottle in her direction.*) Well, perhaps just this once. A very small glass. (*She is trying to be friendly. That is the trouble. He knows she is trying to be friendly.*) Did you see Paul of Yugoslavia?

DAVID

Yes. (*He pours her a glass, which she takes.*)

QUEEN

Does he like being Regent?

DAVID

No.

QUEEN

That's what Marina says.

DAVID

He's worried about Hitler.

QUEEN

We all are.

DAVID

I don't know. It depends what happens, I suppose. Paul's even more worried, and quite rightly, about Stalin.

QUEEN

Stalin? You do surprise me. How was George of Greece?

14

DAVID

He'd rather be back at Brown's Hotel.

QUEEN

Naturally being an exile would give him more freedom, but when Greece voted for a monarchy he had to go back. He had to obey the call of duty. (*The meaning behind her words is not lost on the King. He laughs.*)

DAVID

Well, George is consoled by one thing. He had his fortune told the other day and he was told he'd die of a heart attack.

QUEEN

And he found that consoling?

DAVID

Well, yes. Until he was told that, he was convinced he'd be assassinated.

QUEEN

You didn't go to Venice.

DAVID

Eden thought I shouldn't.

QUEEN

Mussolini is very tiresome.

DAVID

But I agree absolutely. It's idiotic to push him straight into Hitler's arms. It would have been far more useful seeing Mussolini and charming the pants off him than seeing Paul or George or Boris or even Ataturk. .

QUEEN

Charming the what?

DAVID

Pants. Trousers. It's an Americanism.

QUEEN

So I gathered. (*She smiles.*) You're very fond of American expressions. (*She looks at him. He smiles back at her. They both know what is on her mind, what she cannot say.*) Tell me, is it true that Paul of Greece is going to marry Frederica?

DAVID

No. She is going to marry him.

QUEEN

She's very young.

DAVID

And very determined. (*A pause.*)

QUEEN

David—

16

Act One

DAVID

Weren't you at her parents' wedding in Berlin?

QUEEN

Yes, that was the last time I saw the poor old Kaiser and the Tsar. The Tsarina wasn't there. She was ill. As usual. You know she was the greatest single cause of the revolution. By her obsession for Rasputin she made the throne an object for common gossip, and once anyone does that, they are lost. If Carol of Romania goes on behaving as he is doing much longer, he won't last. I'm so glad you decided not to visit him.

DAVID

I'm glad you're pleased, but I wanted to go. My government advised against it and both of you are wrong. All you're concerned about is Carol's morals.

QUEEN

He's treated Helene abominably.

DAVID

What's that got to do with it? Do you know what is going to destroy us? Classical education and Puritan morals. Put a classical education and Puritan morals together and you get a dodo. We're governed by dodos. The only politician who's any good is Churchill and he was useless at Harrow and not even his best friends could call him a Puritan.

QUEEN

And he's never been more unpopular.

DAVID

He's never been more right. It is perfectly obvious what is going to happen. They are terrified in the Balkans and I don't blame them. You see, both the Germans and the Russians want the Danube basin. They're both after the granaries of Hungary, they both want a way into the Mediterranean and once they have that they both want Persian oil, which means they both want to threaten Turkey, Egypt, Suez, India and us. It's as clear as daylight. Now, to meet this threat we need friends and we need military strength. As it is, we have no army, no air force, and an enormous navy composed of obsolete ships without ammunition. Consequently, nobody dares to be our friends.

QUEEN

We are rearming.

DAVID

We're manufacturing one rather small gun a year. The dictators are radiant. (*He picks up the ash tray from the table beside the* QUEEN's *chair.*) May I? (*Taking the ash tray.*) I was questioned most carefully about our rearmament program by Ataturk. I said what I could, of course, and he won't be an enemy; but with an army worth mentioning he'd be our friend.

QUEEN

Why don't you tell Baldwin all this? He's so steady and
sensible.

DAVID

He looks solid and sensible. That's why he gets away
with it all. Actually, he's lazy and narrow-minded. Anyway, at the moment he's on holiday.

QUEEN

Exactly. He's gone abroad. He must see and hear things.

DAVID

How can he, when he's asleep on a deck chair the entire
time? On the rare occasions when he wakes up, he reads
a detective story set in cozy old England, talks to his
wife who resembles nothing so much as a cozy old tea-
pot, then they go into the residents' lounge filled with
cozy old colonels—all British—and drink a cozy old
cup of tea. The one thing you can be certain he never
does is talk to well-informed foreigners.

QUEEN

And what about Eden? He shares your point of view,
doesn't he?

DAVID

Only partially. Anthony is busy conducting his little
duel with Mussolini, which is sheer waste of valuable

time. All he's done is to make him Hitler's ally. If you can see any sense in that course of action, you're cleverer than I am. Sometimes, Mamma, I'd like to impeach the entire cabinet. I'd dismiss them if I thought it would do any good.

QUEEN (*profoundly shocked*)

David!

DAVID

Don't worry, I won't. Apart from anything else, His Majesty's loyal opposition is almost as idiotic as His Majesty's government. All they can talk about is good will among the world's workers, no rearmament whatsoever, and hark back to the General Strike—and where that policy would get us I shudder to think. So I shall continue my own holiday. I'm going to Balmoral.

QUEEN

Oh, good. I am glad. The rest will do you good. From all accounts, your Balkan adventure was far from restful. Though interesting, I'm sure.

DAVID (*carefully*)

I suppose you read a good deal about it in the papers.

QUEEN

A certain amount. The foreign press was, I gather, rather a nuisance.

DAVID

I asked everywhere to be received with the minimum of fuss. Actually, Ataturk was the only one who gave an official reception.

QUEEN

He would. But then he's not a monarch.

DAVID

No. He received us very formally.

QUEEN (*after a deliberate pause*)

Us?

DAVID (*after a tiny hesitation*)

Me and my party.

QUEEN

Oh, yes. Bertie and Elizabeth are already up at Birkhall.

DAVID

Oh, good.

QUEEN

They hope you won't mind, but they've asked Archbishop Lang to stay.

DAVID

They can ask whom they like and why should I mind?

QUEEN

They know you don't care for him.

DAVID

I'm indifferent to him.

QUEEN

I think he was hurt not to be asked by you.

DAVID

He wouldn't have fitted in. George and Marina will be staying with me.

QUEEN

They'll like that. George's so much less wild now he's married.

DAVID

When's her baby due?

QUEEN

December some time. I've been very lucky with all my daughters-in-law so far.

DAVID

Yes. Mamma?

QUEEN

Yes?

Act One

DAVID

Would you like some more sherry?

QUEEN

Not for me. Do help yourself to more, though. (*Pause.*)
Who else have you invited to Balmoral?

DAVID

The Buccleughs, the Roseberys. One or two others.
Some American friends of mine.

QUEEN

On the whole, I don't care for Americans. They're so
loud.

DAVID

I rather like them, Mamma. In fact I like one or two
Americans very much indeed. (*The all-important subject is nearly embarked upon. They look at each other
warily.*)

(FOOTMAN *enters up center.*)

FOOTMAN

Luncheon is served. (*The chance is lost.*)

QUEEN

Shall we go in? It's just ourselves.

CURTAIN

23

SCENE TWO

AT RISE OF CURTAIN: *It is two months later, before dinner.* PRINCESS MARY, *the Princess Royal, comes in up center, followed by* LADY AIRLIE. *The Princess Royal, Countess of Harewood, supports her mother dutifully in all things. She is in her late thirties.*)

MARY

I wanted a word with you before I saw the Queen.

MABELL

Ma'am.

MARY

How is she?

MABELL

Exhausted, I should imagine. Five extra audiences today on top of her usual commitments. She won't put off a single appointment.

MARY

Has anything else happened?

MABELL

I think so. But what exactly I don't know. The telephone has never stopped ringing. The Palace is in absolute turmoil.

MARY

Where is Mamma now?

MABELL

She's dressing for dinner.

MARY

But she's usually dressed long before this.

MABELL

Mr. Baldwin has been on the telephone for over half an hour.

MARY

Good heavens!

MABELL

It must have been important. You know how Her Majesty hates the telephone. For all I know, the Queen may still be talking to him.

MARY

Oh, dear.

MABELL

The whole country is rife with rumors. I'm sure this press silence is unwise.

MARY

Unwise? It's the one thing we're grateful for.

MABELL

In my view, open discussion is preferable to all this speculation. Every M.P. knows, and they all have relatives and friends. The Household all knows. We are none of us without families. Every person who goes abroad knows and comes back spreading further stories. The moment anyone realizes I've recently been to America, they ask me about her. "What are they saying in America? How many times has she been married? Is she a millionairess several times over?" They then go to the other extreme and rush around telling everyone her family was nearly destitute. The truth is the last thing they want to know.

MARY

What is the truth?

MABELL

She comes from a reasonably well-off American family. Her second husband is English and rather well-to-do.

MARY

I've heard she was a debutante before the war.

MABELL

Not over here.

MARY

No, no. In Baltimore.

MABELL

Oh, that's quite different, ma'am, that doesn't count.

MARY

Have you met her?

MABELL

Once.

MARY

Where?

MABELL

Last month at Balmoral.

MARY

Did you like her?

MABELL

Yes, I did. She was exceptionally well-dressed. She was

very witty. I would think her a most sensible woman as
a rule. At the moment I suspect that, after your mother,
she is the most bewildered woman in Britain. I don't
think she knows what is happening to her. The King has
put her into the most terrible predicament.

MARY

He's put us all into a predicament. As a family we have
to be loyal to the Crown, that is to say to the King. But
not only the King. To the whole idea of monarchy as
well. So what do we do now? Be loyal to him personally
or to the Crown as an institution?

MABELL

That is a question we are all facing, the Queen most of
all.

MARY

Have you ever been with the King when he's been un-
expectedly recognized?

MABELL

No.

MARY

I was once. I took him shopping in York. It was my own
fault. I can shop there, as a rule, quite privately and
peacefully. When I was with the King, suddenly he was
recognized. A woman shouted, "It's the Prince of
Wales." A crowd gathered and it took over half an hour

for us to get to the manager's office. Police had to be called and we drove away in state with a motorcycle escort. It must be dreadful to be the object of such adulation all your life. You lose all privacy. All peace. The rest of us—my brothers, me, even my mother—can go about our business in peace. He can't. He never can. I sometimes wonder if he is breaking under the strain— if his lack of wisdom, his impatience, aren't all symptoms of—well—an incipient nervous breakdown? Perhaps I'm talking nonsense.

MABELL

No. I've heard this theory before. Forgive me, ma'am, but I'm not certain I agree with it. After all, what has he done since he's been King? We've had six months' court mourning when public appearances are kept to a minimum. The moment summer came, he was off on the Balkan cruise. True, he made some official visits, but he had whole days at sea in between. There are no cheering crowds in the middle of the Mediterranean. No, ma'am, if I may say so, the King hasn't begun to feel the strain of monarchy yet.

(*The* QUEEN *comes in quickly right.*)

QUEEN

Ah, my dear, thank goodness you are here before David. (MARY *curtsies to her mother, then kisses her.*) He's seen Baldwin. But I can find out nothing.

MABELL

I thought you were speaking to Number Ten just now,
ma'am.

QUEEN

Only to the secretary.

MARY

Harry, my husband—

QUEEN

Yes, dear, yes.

MARY

Well, Mamma, it is confusing having a husband and a
brother called Harry. I had to make clear which Harry
I meant—anyway, he was at the House of Lords and he
heard nothing.

QUEEN

No one knows anything. The family least of all. Did
Mabell tell you about Balmoral?

MARY

Only that Mrs. Simpson had visited there.

QUEEN

You know nothing about Aberdeen, then?

MARY

No.

QUEEN

For six months, at least, he agreed to open a hospital in Aberdeen. At the last moment he canceled.

MARY

Why?

QUEEN

Mourning for Papa, he said. And then, on the very day that he should have opened the hospital, he drives into Aberdeen in his shooting brake to meet her at the station. Of course he was recognized and within minutes Aberdeen was in an uproar. If they had sat and thought about it for months they couldn't have conceived a more foolish course of action.

MARY

Not possibly.

(MARGARET WYNDHAM *enters right.*)

MARGARET

I telephoned Fort Belvedere as you asked, ma'am. His Majesty left some time ago and so he shouldn't be long.

QUEEN

Thank you.

MARGARET

How are you, ma'am?

QUEEN

Splendid, splendid.

MARGARET

Tired, no doubt.

QUEEN

It's been a trying day.

MARGARET

Yes, of course. I do hope this evening won't be too difficult.

QUEEN (*brightly*)

I hope so, too.

MARGARET

It's always darkest before the dawn.

QUEEN

Always.

MABELL

Margaret, dear, are you ready?

MARGARET

Oh, yes.

MABELL

Margaret's dining with me, ma'am. The King will be here soon and we cannot scuttle away like a couple of kitchen-maids the moment he arrives. Your Majesty. Your Royal Highness. (*They curtsy and start to go.*) Oh, ma'am.

QUEEN

Yes.

MABELL

Shall I telephone the Duchess of Gloucester again?

QUEEN

No, no, it's too late. Besides, I couldn't possibly put her off at the last moment.

MABELL

Ma'am. (*Exit up center the two ladies-in-waiting.*)

QUEEN

I like Margaret. I really do. I just wish she wouldn't relish the crisis so much. She talks to me as if I was a hopeless case in a hospital for incurables.

MARY

Anyway, Lady Airlie saved you.

QUEEN

Mabell is wonderful. A tower of strength. And so are you. I couldn't manage without you. Dinner this evening is not going to be much fun. (*At this unaccustomed display of emotion,* MARY *moves away. She is devoted to her mother but, like her, dislikes emotional scenes. The* QUEEN *is in no way rebuffed. She would have done the same.*)

MARY

What's all this about Alice?

QUEEN

Oh, it's too awful. I've done the most dreadful thing. Well, it isn't dreadful, really—it's dreadful of me to say it's dreadful, as I like her so much. Oh, dear, I'm becoming incoherent. It's like living on the edge of Vesuvius. Every morning my hands tremble, literally tremble, as I open my paper. I shall never forgive David for what he's done to us. Never. Even when it's all over I shall never feel quite the same towards him.

MARY

Mamma—

QUEEN

I mean it. Oh, I shall always love him. Always. But to expose us to this ordeal is unforgivable.

35

MARY

He couldn't help falling in love.

QUEEN

He could help this crisis. Did he imagine his choice would be welcomed with open arms?

MARY

He's so in love, I believe he did. (*The* QUEEN *takes a cigarette from box beside her and tries to light it with table lighter.*)

QUEEN

As long as she was married to this—(*Holds lighter out to* MARY.) Please—(MARY *lights her cigarette.*)—poor Mr. Simpson—thank you—he wasn't able to marry her, so there could be no actual constitutional crisis. He could say with impunity that he would brook no interference in his private life. The moment she embarked on these divorce proceedings the situation changed. But he doesn't understand that.

MARY

You've seen him?

QUEEN

No, no. Baldwin's seen him. I've seen Baldwin. The family doesn't exist as far as David's concerned. But about today. First of all, Baldwin telephoned me to say

he was going to Fort Belvedere to see David. And why
is he out there, quite inaccessible? He's absolutely no
consideration. He should be at the Palace. Anyway, then
David telephoned me: Could he come to dinner? I said
"Of course." Would we be alone? I said, did he mind
your being there? He said your being there suited him
admirably. It would help.

MARY

It would help?

QUEEN

Those were his words. So it was all arranged and he
rang off. Then, and only then, I remembered that Alice
was coming to dinner.

MARY

Couldn't you put her off? She won't mind.

QUEEN

I can't find her. Your brother Harry is at some army
camp and Alice has been on an official visit to Worthing.
It might just as well be Mars. I simply could not contact
her. Admittedly I tried for only half an hour, because
then I had Baldwin's secretary on the telephone asking
me to receive the Editor of the *Times* as soon as I could.
Naturally I agreed. Mr. (*Trying to remember the
name.*)—Dawson?

MARY

Yes.

QUEEN

Dawson came around at once and told me the *Times* was being inundated with letters about Mrs. Simpson, all hostile to David.

MARY

Is he going to publish any?

QUEEN

He is not only planning to publish them, he intends to support them with a bitter editorial attack on David. And once that happens, all other papers will join in the fray, the floodgates will be opened and we—the monarchy—will be bang in the middle of a political crisis. The country will be split in two. I implored Dawson to stay his hand, and for the moment he will. He won't publish the letters yet. But that's all he'll say.

(PAGE *enters up center.*)

PAGE

Her Royal Highness, the Duchess of Gloucester.

(*The Duchess of Gloucester enters. Known as* ALICE, *she is attractive, dark and very shy. She curtsies.* PAGE *withdraws.*)

QUEEN

Alice, dear. (*They embrace.*)

38

Act One

ALICE

Mamma. (*She kisses* MARY. *To* QUEEN.) How are you?

QUEEN

I am a little distrait, I fear. I've had a trying day. You must forgive me.

ALICE

Of course. Is there any news?

MARY

Not yet. Have some sherry, Alice?

ALICE

That would be lovely.

MARY

Mamma?

QUEEN

Not for me. Alice, dear, David is coming to dinner.

ALICE

I see.

QUEEN

He asked if he might come and I think wants to talk about business matters. Oh, dear, this is so awkward.

ALICE

It isn't a bit. Obviously it would be far simpler if you and Mary were alone with David.

QUEEN

You're so nice and sensible. I knew you would be. If only David would marry someone like you!

ALICE

I feel so sorry for you over all this.

QUEEN

If you could just make some excuse after dinner, say you're tired and slip away—

ALICE

Wouldn't it be simpler if I escaped now?

QUEEN

No, no. I won't hear of it. I asked you to dinner, and dinner you must have. I refuse to be inhospitable.

(PAGE *enters up center.*)

PAGE

His Majesty.

(DAVID *enters up center, wearing tails, as he is dining*

Act One

with his mother. The women all curtsy. He kisses the
QUEEN's *hand.* PAGE *withdraws.*)

DAVID

Mamma.

QUEEN

I've asked for dinner to be served as soon as you arrived.
I know how busy you are, David; you won't have long
to wait.

DAVID

Thank you, Mamma. (DAVID *glances at* ALICE.)

QUEEN

Poor Alice! She's exhausted. She's been at Worthing all
day and she's asked if you wouldn't mind if she went
straight home after dinner.

DAVID (*with almost audible relief*)

Of course not. Hullo, Mary. How good of you to come.
How are you?

MARY

Lovely to see you. Sherry, David?

DAVID

I am too tired. Is there any whisky?

41

MARY

Yes.

DAVID

If I could have some?

QUEEN

Of course. (*There is a pause.*)

DAVID

Worthing?

ALICE

Yes.

DAVID

That's near Brighton, isn't it?

ALICE

Yes.

MARY

By the sea.

DAVID

It's got a new Town Hall. Did I open it?

QUEEN

No. Georgie did.

DAVID

Why did I think I did?

QUEEN

It was before he was married. He lived in York House with you then. Perhaps that's why. (*There is a pause.*)

MARY

It's so awkward having a brother and a husband called Harry. Don't you find it so, Alice? I find myself saying things like "my husband Harry" or "my brother Harry"—

ALICE

It is awkward. I have a brother called George and a brother-in-law called George also. (*Another pause.*)

QUEEN

Of course, in Queen Victoria's day every branch of the family had to have a daughter called Victoria. It was most confusing.

MARY *and* ALICE

Mm—

DAVID

To say nothing of all the Alberts. (*Pause.*)

43

QUEEN

I'm glad to hear that the outside of Buckingham Palace is to be repainted. It's not before time.

DAVID

Yes. It's for the coronation. (*Dreadful pause.*) I must congratulate you, Mamma. I saw in the *Times* that your favorite charity, the London Needlework Guild, has had a record number of contributions.

QUEEN

Yes. I'm very pleased.

ALICE

You must be.

QUEEN

Dinner, I'm sure, will be very soon.

SLOW CURTAIN

SCENE THREE

AT RISE OF CURTAIN: *After dinner.* (DAVID *is on stage alone. He looks at his watch, goes to window.* MARY *enters up center, shown in by* PAGE.)

DAVID

Oh.

MARY

That was, I think, the most agonizing meal I've ever sat through.

DAVID

I feel so sorry for Alice. I seem to do nothing else but have strained meals with Mamma.

MARY

I don't know what you are planning to say to her now, but do be gentle. She's terribly upset.

DAVID

Yes, I know.

MARY

You know how self-controlled she always is. Well, just before you arrived she almost broke down.

DAVID

Have you ever thought that things would have been far happier for us all if Mamma—just once in her life—had actually broken down? When Papa nearly died in 1928, I know and you know that she was distraught. All she ever said was, "Dear me. It's all very worrying." This spectacular self-control and poise, admirable as it is for public life, is perhaps not quite admirable in private. She loves us. All of us. Even me. But I never really understood that until I was grown up.

MARY

She felt—still feels—that everything has to be sacrificed to the Crown.

DAVID

To Papa.

MARY

And now to you.

DAVID

Not necessarily. Papa never stepped out of line. It seems I do. Papa married when he should have done, fathered several sons, and served in the Navy. He was conventional in every conceivable way. I am not. It was

much easier for her to sacrifice everything for him than
to do so for me.

MARY

She didn't do it alone. He did it too. He wanted a naval
career. He had to give that up when he became Prince
of Wales.

DAVID

Yes, but he had a private life to turn to. He was happy
with Mamma. He was middle-aged when he became
Prince of Wales. I was sixteen. Throughout my life Papa
always told me to remember who I was. Well, who am
I? One day I sat down and worked it out. It's as if I
was the last goldfish in the world. The rest of my breed
has become extinct. I was never just a prince. I was an
heir and now I'm a monarch. No other large empire
remains, so no other royalty has my celebrity value.
Since 1918 I've been a freak.

MARY

I think that's putting it a little strongly.

DAVID

And then I looked at Mamma and Papa. They've been
so busy being parent figures to the nation they've never
had time for us.

MARY

And I think that is putting it far too brutally. David—
you are fond of Mamma?

47

DAVID

Yes. Yes, I am. If I didn't like her, which I do really, this evening would be easy. Instead of which it's going to be hell.

MARY

What is going to happen?

DAVID

I don't know for sure. (*Suddenly he smiles gaily, confidently.*) But I shall win.

MARY (*taken aback*)

Win?

DAVID

You'll see.

MARY

What do you mean?

(PAGE *opens door up center and the* QUEEN *enters.*)

QUEEN

I've told them we won't be having coffee, so we won't be disturbed. Brandy is over there.

DAVID

Thank you. Mamma? Mary?

48

QUEEN

No, thank you.

MARY

No, thank you. (DAVID *pours out his brandy.*)

DAVID

That was a delicious dinner.

QUEEN

I thought you'd like it, so I sent for Mrs. Grant and complimented her.

DAVID

Oh, good. I sent a message to her myself by the page. I can never remember his name.

QUEEN

John.

DAVID

Oh, well. It's a very usual name. (*There is a silence. It is not a hostile silence. It is just that no one knows what to say. His mother and sister are already seated.*) Well. This isn't easy and the trouble is that not only have I so much to tell you that I don't know where to begin, I am uncertain as to how much you already know. (DAVID *has never seemed more touchingly youthful than he does now.*) This is sounding like a prepared speech and I suppose that's what it is. I have rehearsed again and again how to tell you. How much, in fact, do you know?

QUEEN

Nothing for certain.

MARY

We have heard rumors, of course. (DAVID *sits*.)

QUEEN

I wish I could help you to tell me. I wish I could convince you that I am not unsympathetic to your difficulties. My parents were both very excitable people, their emotions were always on the surface. They frequently embarrassed me. Perhaps that has made me reticent about my own feelings. I wish only to help you. You're my son. You're my king.

DAVID

That's the trouble. I cannot be one without the other. I'm in love. (*There is a silence*.) I'm in love with an American woman called Wallis Simpson. She is married to a Mr. Ernest Simpson. They are divorcing. As soon as she is free, I will marry her.

MARY

Marry her, David?

DAVID

Yes, of course. What else can I do? I love her. I must, therefore, marry her.

Act One

QUEEN (*speaking carefully*)

I understand perfectly that having fallen deeply in love, you would wish to marry the object of your affection. But in this instance there are certain difficulties.

DAVID

They can be overcome.

QUEEN

First and foremost, you are Head of the Church.

DAVID

A meaningless title.

QUEEN

Not to the general public.

MARY

It may be a meaningless title in Mayfair. It's not where I live, in Yorkshire. Or anywhere else in the country. David, as Mrs. Simpson will be divorced—has already been divorced, I understand, from a previous husband —how can you marry her?

QUEEN

Mary has put the position perfectly. It is impossible for you to marry her. Surely you understand that?

DAVID

Unfortunately I do not.

51

QUEEN

But, David—

DAVID

It is impossible for me, with the Church ruling on divorce as it now stands, and in my present position, to marry a divorced woman.

QUEEN

Well then?

DAVID

But rulings—even Church rulings—can be changed if necessary and my position altered. One or the other will have to be done.

QUEEN

Both are impossible and what's more—

DAVID

Let me finish, Mamma. I know you will find this difficult to believe and Archbishop Lang would be amazed, but I am not without religious scruples. If I were, there would be no problem.

QUEEN

Dearest boy, I accept that absolutely. What I am unable to accept is the form your religion takes when it allows you even to contemplate marriage to a divorced woman.

DAVID

You do realize, Mamma, that there is nothing to stop me

marrying Wallis tomorrow in a civil ceremony, the moment she is free, and if I had no respect for religion, nothing to prevent me from being crowned before she was my wife.

QUEEN

I realize that only too well.

DAVID

Very well, then. So you must understand that if there is a crisis, it is not because I am lacking in serious principles, but because—*because* my religion means a great deal to me. Lang and everyone else in authority equate religion with solemnity. I do not. Surely it is possible to enjoy life and even seem frivolous and still feel deeply about religion.

QUEEN

No one doubts the depth of your feelings.

DAVID

But you do. You all do.

MARY

Whom do you mean by "all"?

DAVID

Lang, Baldwin, everyone. I find the Church of England, like the present government, increasingly out of touch. And just as they underestimate my religious feelings, so they underestimate my desire for marriage. It is essential for me to marry the woman I love. Not just in a civil ceremony, but in church.

MARY

But how can you expect the Church to bless your marriage?

DAVID

It must change its laws or else my position must be changed.

QUEEN

David, David, David! Please believe me when I say I sympathize with you. I really do. But we must be realistic. Now I am the first to agree that you never had a chance to settle down. There was the war. Then those long Empire tours, following one after the other. I said at the time they were a mistake. I said as much to your father.

DAVID (*surprised*)

Did you?

QUEEN

Oh, yes. And to Mr. Baldwin, too. Oh, I know you did a splendid job. Many people think you held the Empire together. But it gave you no chance to build a life, to settle down.

DAVID

No.

Act One

QUEEN (*with warm sympathy—she feels she is getting through to him*)
I really do understand how much you want to marry and I'm sure Mrs. Simpson is charming. I know George and Marina like her very much, so do the Mountbattens.

DAVID
Oh, Mamma. I love her so much.

QUEEN
I'm sure you do. (*They are closer than perhaps they have ever been. The* QUEEN *continues.*) But however much you love her and however charming she is, as your wife, as your queen, she is out of the question. (*The* QUEEN *had thought the King was weakening and he had thought she was. He stares at her aghast whilst she continues gently, calmly but relentlessly.*) You have your duty to do as King. You must give her up.

DAVID
Why? (*For the first time his voice betrays his inner agitation. His disappointment is echoed by her. Their voices start to rise.*)

QUEEN
She's been divorced.

DAVID
There's no other reason?

55

QUEEN

What other reason could there be?

DAVID

You know nothing against her?

QUEEN

Other than the divorce, no.

DAVID

She's not a criminal, for example. An alcoholic, perhaps?

QUEEN

David.

DAVID

I can marry with the Church's approval a criminal alcoholic, but the Church will not allow me to marry a divorced woman.

QUEEN

David, there is nothing to be gained by getting excited and talking wildly. The Church would have no reason to oppose your marriage to a criminal alcoholic. The government would intervene. To the vast majority of us—a marriage is for a lifetime. Now I understand that this is a fact you find unpalatable. Nevertheless it exists and you must face it.

DAVID

Wallis' first husband drank; their marriage became a mockery.

QUEEN

I don't know the American form of marriage service, but presumably she took him for better or worse.

DAVID

She left him for a time, then went back to him and tried again. Having failed with him twice, she finally decided on a divorce. She was the innocent party.

QUEEN

I'm sure that's all true. I understand that with her second divorce she's again the innocent party. But divorce itself is what is wrong.

DAVID

Not in my view.

QUEEN

The Church's teaching is quite clear.

DAVID

The Church's teaching was laid down by men specially dedicated to a spiritual life, on top of which not one of its present leaders has the remotest understanding of the twentieth century.

QUEEN

Be that as it may—

DAVID

Furthermore, do you realize that the marriage vow is the only unbreakable contract? You can cease to be a clergyman; the Roman Catholic church will release nuns and monks from their vows. Only a husband and wife are to be tied together in permanent misery.

QUEEN

David, as a constitutional monarch you can act only within the government's wishes and in this instance the government supports the Church.

DAVID

Only where I'm concerned. Civil remarriage for everyone else is perfectly legal and respectable.

QUEEN

You are in a unique position. You have to pay a unique price for it. You cannot have the privileges of your position without its responsibilities. Mr. Baldwin has explained this to you. You seem to understand no one's point of view but your own. As head of the Church—

DAVID

The Church is wrong and in my view uncharitable and unchristian on this issue of divorce and remarriage.

QUEEN

Nevertheless, the government—

DAVID

Nevertheless, the government, incapable of a coherent foreign policy or of a constructive home policy for that matter, is prepared to be firm only on a matter of hypocritical virtue.

MARY

David! You are quite right when you say the Royal Marriages Act does not apply to you as monarch. The moment Mrs. Simpson is free you can certainly legally marry her. The press—despite all the gossip, the press in Britain is still silent—

QUEEN

—for the time being—

MARY

—but once they know you plan to marry her, how can they continue to be silent about her then? The King's bride will be an object of legitimate interest. Her past will become public property.

DAVID (*icily*)

What do you mean, her past?

MARY

We all have a past. When George married Marina, the

entire Greek family history was in all the papers. When any of us marries, this happens. It's a fact we have to live with.

QUEEN

Exactly.

MARY

The press cannot fail to mention her former marriages, her divorces. The public will want to know when and how you met her. They will see that she divorced Mr. Simpson in 1936 and married you in 1937. They will realize that you knew her, fell in love with her when she was still married to another man. The people of this country are fundamentally moral and they will disapprove most strongly of such a marriage. Consequently they will disapprove of you and your wife and however nice she is, however much you love her, such a state of affairs can only do the Throne damage.

DAVID

Temporarily.

QUEEN

We cannot be sure of that. It could be lasting damage.

MARY

David, Mamma and I are concerned for your happiness. But we are royal. We are also concerned for the Throne.

QUEEN

It is impossible—impossible, David—for any king of England, any son of mine, brought up as he has been in the tradition of service to his country, to put the Throne in danger.

DAVID

There is absolutely no question of that. The Throne has been damaged temporarily before, yet it survives. My predecessors—

QUEEN

Your predecessors lived in an age when republicanism was not at all common in other countries. Now it is. We are the only major power still a monarchy.

DAVID

I intend that we shall remain not only a monarchy but also a major power.

QUEEN

Then, David, my dear boy, what are we arguing about? Your duty is clear.

DAVID

We are now coming to the real point. You see, if I raised the religious issue of my marriage, it wasn't just from my own selfish viewpoint, but because I believe the Church of England must become more modern.

QUEEN

Modern?

DAVID

Up to date. We must all become up to date. The whole
country. We cannot hope to stay a major power unless
we do. I believe in evolution, Mamma, and not revolution. But if we do not evolve, and with some speed too,
we will face revolution.

QUEEN

Have you already forgotten our Silver Jubilee? It was
only last year. We were overwhelmed with demonstra-
tions of affection.

DAVID

Towards you and Papa personally but not for the exist-
ing system.

QUEEN

The Throne has never been stronger.

DAVID

And the country never weaker. The Throne is strong because it changes and the country is weak because it
won't.

QUEEN

The Throne has never changed.

DAVID

Of course it has. You changed it. So did Papa. Victoria changed it. She made it respectable when her uncles had made it scandalous.

QUEEN

That's quite true, but—

DAVID

Grandpapa made it gay, social and continental when his mother's old age had made it provincial.

QUEEN

It was never provincial.

DAVID

She never visited London at all. She spent her life in Balmoral and Osborne and that is all. Papa made it British when before it had seemed German. And I—I must be allowed to change it, too.

QUEEN

May one ask how?

DAVID

People say that I don't want to be king, but I do. Would I have worked so hard as Prince of Wales if I didn't? I want to bring the monarchy into the twentieth century. I want to stay on the throne—but on or off the throne

I will marry Mrs. Simpson. (*Pause. He has said it. The bomb has exploded.*)

QUEEN

What did you say? On or off the Throne?

DAVID

That's what I said, Mamma.

QUEEN

Mary—

MARY

Mamma, dear.

QUEEN

Are you serious?

DAVID

Perfectly.

QUEEN

Oh, no—no. I know you are headstrong and stubborn but not even you could be so silly. Yes. Silly. If you feel so strongly about reform of the Church, dealing with unemployment and the international situation, it is your duty to stay on the throne and advise the government accordingly. All your arguments, every single one of them, are arguments for staying on the throne. Not for running away. Cannot you see that? David, you can influence any government, but behind the scenes. That is your right. That is your duty. Your duty. You must be patient. It will take time.

DAVID

If I don't fight over this private issue, it will be over a public one and that would be far, far worse. Don't you see that by making it over a personal issue I am avoiding a major conflict between the government and me?

QUEEN

But you must surely understand that you must never come into open conflict with the government at all.

DAVID

I understand that perfectly. That is why I am trying to contain our disagreement. I am a man as well as a king and I must marry Wallis Simpson. I have told Baldwin this.

QUEEN

And? . . .

DAVID

He advises, so far unofficially, against it. So I have two choices. To give her up and stay on the throne or to marry her and abdicate.

QUEEN

Then only one answer is possible. You must give her up.

It must be terrible to love someone you cannot marry. But I will help you. The family will help you.

DAVID

I have chosen to abdicate. So you see there will be no open conflict. You see, Mamma, there is something you do not understand in all this. I cannot live without her. Not a day. Not an hour. I've known more beautiful women and more charming women. I must have done, because I know when I first met her I thought her neither the one nor the other. But to me she is the most fascinating woman in the world. Her gaiety, her curiosity about life, constantly delights. To me she has also become more beautiful and more charming than anyone else alive. When I'm with her I am rich and fulfilled. When I'm away from her I feel only half alive. She gives my life significance. Without her it is quite pointless. So I didn't hesitate a moment when Baldwin advised me not to marry her. I said at once, "Very well, I'm prepared to abdicate."

MARY (*at length*)

What about us?

DAVID

Us?

QUEEN

What about the family?

66

Act One

DAVID

Well, what about it?

QUEEN

What is going to happen to the Throne?

DAVID

Bertie will succeed. He'll do it very well, really. He's what you all want. He'll do exactly as he's told. After all, he always has.

QUEEN

You are prepared to abdicate—to desert your post?

DAVID (*sharply*)

I cannot be King unless I am married to Wallis.

QUEEN

To desert your post, deny your duty.

DAVID (*with great emphasis*)

I am fully prepared to work and work hard at being King, but I must be allowed the fundamental right of every male in the world. To marry the woman I love. You all wonder if she's good enough for me. I wonder if I am good enough for her. Mamma, you would understand my whole attitude and why I feel as I do if you would meet her. Will you receive her? Will you see her?

QUEEN

You feel strongly about divorce and remarriage. So do
I. My views are the exact opposite to yours. I cannot
change now. No. I cannot receive her.

DAVID

Mary?

MARY

I agree with Mamma.

DAVID

Wallis made two mistakes in her life. And a Christian
society cannot forgive her for them.

QUEEN

If you stayed on the throne, if you did your duty, you
could change that society.

DAVID

But you see, I'd only succeed with her by my side. That
is what no one understands. Not even she does. Wallis
is your strongest ally, Mamma. She wants me to stay.
She wants me to give her up. But I won't. Not now.
Not ever. If the only way I can marry her is by abdicating, then I shall abdicate with joy. (*He turns and walks
out of the room as:*)

THE CURTAIN FALLS

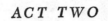

ACT TWO

SCENE ONE

AT RISE OF CURTAIN: *It is now a fortnight later in early December. It is late morning. The* QUEEN *is talking to* MR. MONCKTON, K.C., *a dark, attractive man of about forty. He is charming, wears glasses and is very able.*)

QUEEN

But surely you understand, Mr. Monckton, that the present state of affairs cannot go on much longer. The King must reach a decision soon. A fortnight ago he said in this very room that he wanted to abdicate. What is going on?

MONCKTON

You must remember, ma'am, that until very recently His Majesty was the most advised man in the world. Now, in this supreme crisis of his life, apart from Mrs. Simpson, he has no one. His government, his court, even his family, are all opposed to him. So he has turned to his personal friends for advice, and surely this is reasonable, ma'am?

QUEEN

On the face of it, yes. But who has he turned to? You, Mr. Monckton, I know, are a man of great good sense.

All of us are fortunate that you have agreed to act as intermediary between the King and his cabinet. But what about the others? What about Churchill? What about Beaverbrook? They are anxious, not so much to help the King, as to attack Baldwin. You must know that as well as I do.

MONCKTON

Churchill is a born cavalier. He sees his loyalty to the King in terms of high romance. Beaverbrook may want to attack Baldwin but it doesn't matter if he does, as the King is determined to behave with constitutional correctness.

QUEEN

You mean he doesn't take their advice either.

MONCKTON

That would be one way of putting it.

QUEEN

He never would listen to anyone.

MONCKTON

Ma'am, the King's friends are all urging delay. But the only advice he wants is how to stay on the throne and still marry Mrs. Simpson.

QUEEN

But surely his friends all realize the nation will never accept her as queen?

Act Two

MONCKTON

She needn't become queen. (*Long pause.*)

QUEEN

Mr. Monckton, you're not seriously suggesting a morganatic marriage?

MONCKTON

It's the only loophole open to him. A few days ago Esmond Harmsworth took Mrs. Simpson to Claridge's for lunch and put it to her that she could become the King's wife without becoming queen. (*The* QUEEN *looks at* MR. MONCKTON.) After all, ma'am, European royal families did it quite often.

QUEEN

And they were always disastrous.

MONCKTON

Franz Ferdinand's was a happy marriage, ma'am.

QUEEN

No doubt. But it was a source of constant embarrassment to everyone, and it split the imperial family in two. What does the King think of the idea?

MONCKTON

He considers it distasteful but a possible solution.

QUEEN

It's quite impossible. For him to contemplate it at all

makes one despair all over again. I called you in to discover what has been going on, Mr. Monckton, and you have confirmed my worst fears. His secretary, Alec Hardinge, sent him a perfectly reasonable letter suggesting Mrs. Simpson leave the country, warning him of the impending crisis and telling him quite properly that the government might call an election to be fought over his proposed marriage. And what does the King do? He flies into a terrible rage and refuses to see or even speak to Alec Hardinge.

MONCKTON

I don't think it was a reasonable letter, ma'am. It was far too brutally worded. It put the government's point of view so exactly it might have come from Baldwin's secretary instead of from his own. To suggest that Mrs. Simpson leave the country was a fatal mistake and would only make the King furious. His courtiers have been most unwise in their handling of the monarch. They have made the grave mistake of making it plain that they disapprove of him, and what employer would like that from his employees? On top of which, they have allowed their dislike of Mrs. Simpson to reach the point of venom. Do you know that some of his staff and their wives refer to her as "the kitchen maid"?

QUEEN

No. I didn't know. It is most unfortunate. Most unkind.

MONCKTON

It's worse than that, ma'am. It's disloyal.

74

QUEEN

Mr. Monckton, his court may have been stupid and
snobbish. I don't believe any of them are disloyal.
You must remember, they are concerned not just for
the King himself but also for the Throne. The Throne
is more important than its occupant.

MONCKTON

Those are Mrs. Simpson's sentiments, too.

QUEEN

Then why doesn't she give him up?

MONCKTON

She can't. She wants to leave. He won't let her. In his
present frame of mind he's capable of following her in a
battleship to China.

QUEEN

That I can well believe. Please sit down, Mr. Monckton.

MONCKTON

Ma'am. (*He sits.*)

QUEEN

Clearly the love he has for her is no ordinary love. I met
her once, you know. At a reception we gave for the
Duchess of Kent before her marriage. My son submitted
a list of guests, so of course, along with the rest of his

75

list, she had to be invited. I can remember nothing about her. I cannot recall even what she looks like.

MONCKTON

She's an extremely nice woman. I like her very much indeed. She's calm, sensible and discreet. But what woman, in her present position, wouldn't make a few mistakes? She's more than the wonderful society hostess she's always called. She's kind and thoughtful. She's also quite without personal ambition.

QUEEN

Without ambition?

MONCKTON

Personal ambition, yes. The stories about her being an unscrupulous adventuress bear no relationship to fact at all. Of course she'd be very ambitious for her husband. It may sound ironic, but she has a profound respect for marriage.

QUEEN

With two divorces. Really?

MONCKTON

Oh, yes. She expects her marriage to be ideally happy and her husband to be a success and she will work very hard to achieve both those aims. She's constantly described to me as the driving force behind this. She's not at all. The King wanted her to divorce Simpson—when

Mr. Baldwin asked him to stop the divorce, of course he refused. The King knows they are thought immoral and it infuriates him. He's passionately moral. So is she. It would be easy for them both to be immoral; with a little discretion this immorality would be winked at. *That* is why he's been indiscreet. He has deliberately dragged her round Europe, deliberately given dinner parties for her, so as to make a discreet love affair between them absolutely impossible.

QUEEN

You're a remarkably eloquent advocate, Mr. Monckton. I hope the King and Mrs. Simpson appreciate you. The fact remains that whatever his motives, my son has outraged the Church, the government, his court, all of his relations and world opinion. But tell me, Mr. Monckton, if Mrs. Simpson is a sensible woman, why didn't she stop my son deliberately parading her?

MONCKTON

May I ask, ma'am, have you ever tried to stop the King from doing anything? I've known him since Oxford and I certainly can't. I implored His Majesty to wait a while before he put the morganatic marriage idea to Mr. Baldwin, but he absolutely insists on going ahead.

QUEEN

But if he does that, the Prime Minister will be bound to put it to the Cabinet and then this whole business will become official.

MONCKTON

I'm afraid so.

QUEEN

I've tried to help and guide my son. Quite without success. You will stay with him, Mr. Monckton.

MONCKTON

Yes, of course, ma'am.

QUEEN

He's going to need your help.

MONCKTON

I think I should warn you, ma'am. The press will have to break its silence soon.

QUEEN

And then God alone knows what will happen. As I look into the future, Mr. Monckton, I am filled with foreboding.

THE CURTAIN FALLS

SCENE TWO

AT RISE OF CURTAIN: *It is late in the evening two days later.* MARGARET *is found on stage reading a newspaper. Several others are at her feet. These have enormous banner headlines.* MARGARET *is reading with a certain gusto.* MABELL *comes in right. When she sees what* MARGARET *is doing she is almost openly irritated.*)

MABELL

Oh, Margaret, do put those papers away. The Yorks have arrived.

MARGARET

It's all simply dreadful. Crowds outside the palace have been shouting "God save the King from Baldwin."

MABELL

People should know better.

(PAGE *opens door and the Duchess of York* [ELIZABETH], *followed by the Duke* [BERTIE], *comes in. The Duke, two years younger than his brother, is shy and retiring, with a stammer which becomes pronounced in moments*

79

of stress. He is, however, also very tough when he has to be. His shy, quiet manner is deceptive. The Duchess, thirty-six, is pretty and slightly plump. Formerly Lady Elizabeth Bowes-Lyon, she is now quite used to being royalty and normally, from all accounts, quite extraordinarily charming. She is very distressed, upset and even angry. At first she is controlled; later, for what may have been the only time in her life, her distress causes her anger to break out.)

ELIZABETH

Lady Airlie.

MABELL

Your Royal Highness. (MABELL *and* MARGARET *curtsy. The Duchess and* MABELL *are old friends, so they kiss as they do so. The Duke talks to* MARGARET.)

BERTIE

How is Mamma?

MARGARET

Oh, wonderful as ever, sir. Perfectly calm, but of course very worried. I'll tell her you're here.

BERTIE

If you would. (MARGARET *exits right.*)

ELIZABETH

Is the Queen very distressed?

MABELL

Oh, yes. These dreadful papers were a terrible shock.

ELIZABETH

It's difficult to know which one is worst. I am still very, very upset. We arrived from Scotland this morning totally unprepared for this deluge of publicity. Why were we not warned by the Palace?

BERTIE

They may not have known, darling.

ELIZABETH

Papers come out in the early morning, Bertie. Why wasn't a signal sent to the train? At Euston we were greeted by what seemed to be every cameraman in London and huge newspaper placards shrieking "The King and Mrs. Simpson." (*She sits.*) I don't think, Lady Airlie, that I shall ever be able to hear the words "Mrs. Simpson" without a shudder. (*She laughs.*) Actually, it was rather funny. We went to some reception and the butler announced "The Bishop of Kensington and Mrs. Simpson." The room absolutely froze. And in walked the bishop and on his arm was his amiable wife.

BERTIE

That was the first indication we had that the secret was no longer a secret. Is the King here yet?

MABELL

No, sir.

ELIZABETH

But he is coming?

MABELL

He said so.

BERTIE

Mamma wanted us here first, darling.

(*The* QUEEN *comes in right.*)

QUEEN

Thank goodness you're both here. Elizabeth, my dear.

BERTIE

Mamma. (*He bows, kisses her hand, then embraces her warmly. As he does so,* ELIZABETH *curtsies, then also embraces her.*)

QUEEN

Dear Bertie. (MABELL *goes tactfully to the door, curtsies and withdraws.*)

BERTIE

Mamma, have you any news?

QUEEN

Only what I read in those dreadful newspapers. I sent David an urgent message and he's coming round after ten, he said.

ELIZABETH

Why so late?

QUEEN

I've no idea. I'm in the dark. I'm never off the telephone, yet nobody knows anything. She has, I gather, at last left the country.

ELIZABETH

Yes, but too late. When Alec Hardinge suggested it three weeks ago, it might have done some good—but not now.

QUEEN

David wouldn't let her go. It was only because he was frightened for her safety that he agreed now to her going. You've both got to understand one thing—he loves her. He loves her with all the passion of a boy in his first youth.

ELIZABETH

Yes, but he's not in his first youth. He's forty-two.

BERTIE

I would be very grateful if someone would explain the situation. We hear vaguely from Number Ten, from you, but never from Fort Belvedere. Never David. Of course, we've been in Scotland.

ELIZABETH

There are, I believe, telephones in Fort Belvedere. And please correct me if I'm wrong, but I'm sure it's possible to ring up Scotland from Windsor Great Park.

BERTIE (*soothingly*)

David is under great strain, darling.

ELIZABETH

And so are you. No one seems to understand that, least of all David. You are under great strain. If he deserts his post you would have to take over.

BERTIE

He would never dream of doing a thing like that. B-Baldwin's warnings were merely routine. I'm sure it won't happen. It can't. If that's what's making you so upset, I'm sure you're being upset about nothing. I know David. The government knows him. They know that in him they have a first-rate king and they wouldn't let him go. You'll see. No, what distresses me in this is that I am his heir, his brother, and I would like to help him —somehow. I just wish he wouldn't ignore me.

Act Two

ELIZABETH

Darling Bertie. (*It is clear that this is a love match. For a moment they might have been alone; they are talking quietly to each other.*)

QUEEN (*suddenly and sharply*)

It's not out of the question.

BERTIE (*surprised*)

Hm?

QUEEN

It's not impossible. Your taking over. It's not at all impossible. The government will let him go. They are at loggerheads over everything. The impossible is happening. It shouldn't be. But it is. That is why I wanted you here before David. To tell you what you are up against. Mr. Baldwin's warnings were not routine. They were meant. (*The shock to* BERTIE *and* ELIZABETH *is terrible. They stare appalled at the* QUEEN. *Clearly, whatever may have been told them before, they had refused to accept. Now they believe it.* BERTIE *is like a prisoner who, told repeatedly by his lawyer that he will get a heavy sentence, refuses to believe it and then nearly dies of shock when he gets it. He can hardly speak. She holds him. When* BERTIE *speaks, the stammer becomes pronounced.*)

BERTIE

Why do you think David will d-desert?

85

QUEEN

Because he believes his duty to Mrs. Simpson is greater than his duty to his country.

ELIZABETH

When is he going?

QUEEN

I've no idea. (*They stare at her horrified.*) You have been in Scotland. A country composed of relatively sane people. I have been inhabiting Cloud Cuckoo Land where there are no answers to any question except another question. You say you should have been warned. Of course you should have been. But what are we to say to you? And it's all so simple. You either do your duty or you don't.

BERTIE

What am I going to do, Elizabeth? I've not been trained to be k-king.

(PAGE *enters up center.*)

PAGE

His Majesty.

(DAVID *enters.* PAGE *exits. The* QUEEN's *greeting is definitely cool. He kisses her hand.* BERTIE *gets up and bows.* ELIZABETH *curtsies.*)

Act Two

DAVID

Mamma. Bertie. How was Scotland, Elizabeth?

QUEEN

We are anxious for news, David.

DAVID

Yes, I know. (*The strain is telling. His charm is less overwhelming, his voice sharper.*) There is nothing definite to tell you.

QUEEN

You have seen the papers?

DAVID

Naturally.

QUEEN

I find them extremely disturbing.

DAVID

No more than we do, I assure you. Wallis was appalled.

QUEEN

Are you going to abdicate?

DAVID

Nothing is settled. You have urged so strongly. Naturally, I am trying to remain.

87

QUEEN

If you are set on marrying this—then obviously you cannot remain.

DAVID

You may refer to Wallis by her Christian name or by her present surname which is Mrs. Simpson.

QUEEN

I do not know the lady, so naturally I cannot refer to her by her Christian name.

DAVID

The fact that you do not know her is not her fault. Nor is it mine.

QUEEN

David, I know how devoted you are to Mrs. Simpson.

DAVID

I've had to send her abroad, you know.

QUEEN

Yes, dear, I know. I assure you I do not mean to add to your obvious distress. However, we—the family, your family—are distressed, too. (BERTIE *is visibly distressed.*)

BERTIE

Why are we told nothing? (ELIZABETH *is standing*

slightly away from the rest of them. Hearing her husband's stammer, she glances at him. She is absolutely still and silent.)

DAVID

Because I wish to keep you all out of it. This is not a fight between the whole royal family and Parliament, nor is it about the principle of monarchy and Parliament, but between me and the Cabinet, me and Baldwin. If you were any of you to become involved, particularly you, Bertie, you would be an ally of mine and should I fail, then it would not be just my failure, but your failure, too—the whole family's failure.

QUEEN

Fail at what—

DAVID

In my fight with Baldwin. Do you realize he won't take this to Parliament? Parliament has not been consulted. He won't even let me broadcast. And why? Because he knows there's a body of opinion in my favor. He wants to present Parliament with a *fait accompli* which Churchill says is unconstitutional.

QUEEN

When was Churchill ever right about anything? Look at India and the Dardanelles. His support is of no value to you. And in this instance everybody supports the Prime Minister absolutely. Mr. Attlee supports him.

Can't you see that by refusing to put it openly to Parliament, the Prime Minister is protecting you? Protecting the Crown from becoming a point of political controversy. You should be grateful to him. If the Crown becomes a point of controversy, it will lose its entire value. We are the center of affection. We are the heart of the nation. We are a rallying point in national disaster. No president, no prime minister, can fill that role, and you are destroying us.

DAVID

How can I be when I have removed the argument from any possible political controversy?

QUEEN

But to argue *at all* with your Prime Minister and to have the argument made public is in itself making the Crown controversial.

DAVID

No. I am a point of controversy. Not the Crown.

QUEEN

You cannot separate the two. Nobody can.

DAVID (*quietly and patiently*)
I am prepared to go. I stated that clearly. Right?

QUEEN

Yes.

DAVID

So if I am prepared to go—should the government wish me to go—then there is no conflict. I have agreed. How can there be conflict?

QUEEN

So you are definitely going?

DAVID

Oh, no.

QUEEN

David, dear. I am growing old. I speak German and French and Italian. Double Dutch I never mastered.

DAVID

I said I was *prepared* to go. I did not say I *wanted* to go. There was no hint of a desire to go in my choice of words.

QUEEN

Dear David, in uttering them at all, you abdicated— and you never even knew it. I don't think you understand anything.

BERTIE

If you go—David, what is going to happen?

DAVID

You will take over, of course. What else?

ELIZABETH

I was waiting for that.

QUEEN

If you stay and marry Mrs. Simpson, what will happen? You won't have a government. Mr. Baldwin will resign. His entire cabinet will resign. Mr. Attlee won't take over. The Labour Party disapproves of your proposed marriage quite as bitterly as I do. The working class woman is a respectable woman. She is used to having one husband and sticking to him.

ELIZABETH

I agree.

QUEEN

You won't have an Archbishop of Canterbury. Not one bishop will attend your coronation. Oh, I daresay you'll be able to persuade some renegade clergyman to crown you and I daresay to marry you, but it will be a public humiliation and a mockery of all the Throne stands for. So you will have no government on the one hand and will be at loggerheads with the Church on the other. May I ask, do you propose to become a dictator? And a pope?

DAVID

No, Mamma.

QUEEN

Really, we might as well be living in Romania. Let me make one thing clear to you. Even if you should succeed in staying on your own impossible conditions, in no circumstances whatsoever will I receive Mrs. Simpson.

DAVID

Not even if I marry her morganatically?

QUEEN

Not even then. Never. Never as long as I live. Monarchy symbolizes the family. It is that which gives us our strength. We are born, we marry, we die as a family. A wife shares in every way her husband's position. A morganatic marriage in which Mrs. Simpson is your wife but not your queen strikes at the whole principle of family life; it'll never work. The cabinet can only reject the idea.

DAVID

And if she did become queen? What would you do then?

QUEEN

I have lived my life on certain principles which I know you deplore and consider narrow-minded, and I will not abandon them now. I will never receive her nor attend any function which she attends.

DAVID

I am sorry you have ranged yourself with my enemies, but I expected nothing else. Neither you nor Papa could ever miss an opportunity to criticize me.

QUEEN

That is not true.

DAVID

I have a royal memory too and can quote examples at length if you so desire. But I'm as dedicated as you are to the monarchial system and I have no wish to abdicate. What I am striving to do is to find a formula by which I can stay *and* at the same time marry Wallis Simpson.

ELIZABETH

You could give her up.

DAVID

Could I? You are happily married, Elizabeth. Could you give up Bertie?

ELIZABETH

We are already married. It's not the same.

DAVID

It's the same to me.

94

Act Two

ELIZABETH

And when we married we did not divide the country.

DAVID

You married Bertie because you loved him and I trust you have stayed married for the same reason.

ELIZABETH

I waited some time, months if not years, before I was certain, and being certain, I then made vows which to me mean a great deal. I would never have made them if I hadn't meant to keep them. All married people make these vows of their own free will. No one forces us to do so. Wallis Simpson has made them twice and broken them twice.

QUEEN

To do so once may be allowed in the most terrible of circumstances but to break your marriage vow twice, to divorce twice, is unforgivable.

ELIZABETH

Naturally I sympathize with your desire to escape. I was myself reluctant to become royal.

DAVID

I have no desire to escape.

95

ELIZABETH

It's in everything you say and do.

DAVID

You are reading into my words what's not and has never been there.

QUEEN

You are putting your personal wishes before your duty to your country. The Throne asks for the supreme sacrifice in time of war, a sacrifice millions of men make. It is inconceivable to me how you can accept such a sacrifice from them, yet refuse a far lesser one in return.

DAVID

I don't mind dying for my country. What I refuse to do is live in misery for my country. No one is asked to do that.

QUEEN

You know I was engaged first of all to your father's elder brother. If he had lived, marriage to him would not have been at all easy. It was made clear to me where my duty lay so I agreed to marry him.

DAVID

Oh, yes, I know, but either way you would have had a private life and children. I have none. Nor can you know how such a marriage would have affected you. It might even have made you tolerant.

ELIZABETH

The truth of the matter is that you are convinced that our sacrifices in the name of duty are always unimportant compared to yours. Bertie's sacrifices have been endless and he makes them cheerfully without complaint. On top of which he's had to fight ill-health and a stammer. None of this interests you in the slightest. The only things which concern you are your own emotions. I've heard all about your plans for bringing us into the twentieth century. They can't mean much to you, as without a thought you are prepared to endanger them. The weight of opinion against you is overwhelming. Yet you are so vain—

DAVID (*interrupting*)
Yes—all right—thank you—

ELIZABETH (*continuing without stopping*)
—that not for one moment do you think this opinion could be right and you wrong.

DAVID

O.K., "weight of opinion" is the correct expression. There's Baldwin about to retire from an inglorious career at the end of which our country is defenseless. Lang, whom you all admire, nauseates me with his unctuous hypocrisy, and I wonder if there's a bishop

97

under sixty? The Church, if it continues its present lamentable career, will soon be so out of touch it'll become extinct. The Labour Party is led by elderly Trade Unionists and desiccated dons who can read Latin and Greek fluently but have never seen a Hungarian close to and aren't sure where Belgrade is. But there are young people in this country. Young people who will take over, who reject these outmoded codes of behavior. Must the Crown always be a backwater of fossilized opinion?

BERTIE

All this passion is very fine. But what is happening now?

DAVID

Now? I am striving to stay on the throne. It is a private personal difference of opinion between me and Baldwin. That's why I live at the Fort, my private home, all this time.

ELIZABETH

What will happen if you are told to go?

DAVID

I'll go. And naturally Bertie, as my heir, will take over.

ELIZABETH

Just like that.

DAVID

If I died that's what would happen.

ELIZABETH

Death is not deliberate. This act of yours will be. Bertie
is unprepared. You knew for twenty-six years you
would be king. You have always taken Bertie for
granted and without the slightest consideration you
take him for granted now. We have two children whom
we hope to bring up in reasonable privacy. Now, if you
go, we'll have to bring them up in a glare of ghastly
publicity. And if you dislike being king, do you imagine
Bertie will enjoy it? You are prepared to put a burden
you regard as intolerable on to your own brother's
shoulders.

DAVID

I regard it as intolerable only because I'm not married.
He is.

ELIZABETH

This past year has been a hell on earth for all your
court, your relations, your mother and for Bertie and
me. We have been through the tortures of the damned
in Scotland these past weeks, having to go to endless
functions, told nothing by you, rumors, whispers sur-
rounding us—

DAVID

I was keeping you out of it.

ELIZABETH

We have as much at stake as you have. More. We will

have to clear up the mess. When did you get the papers this morning?

DAVID

First thing.

ELIZABETH

We were in the train. Why didn't you get a message to us? You knew it would be an appalling shock to Bertie. Yet, you could allow us to arrive at Euston to a blaze of publicity with placards screaming your name. Oh, you will career around the country putting on a tremendous show of concern for the poor, but nothing is to be allowed to interfere with your dream of happiness. You can't sit at a desk and read State papers.

DAVID

That's all anybody can think of. State papers. My father read them all and Baldwin did as he liked and we are in a mess.

QUEEN

Your father was a conscientious monarch. How dare you suggest otherwise!

ELIZABETH

As for your plans for the future of this country, they sound like a nightmare. Everybody divorcing everybody. You say you want to reign, but on your terms. You say you wish to be a constitutional king and will act only through the government. But it has to agree with you. You say the Church is out of touch, but only now do you say it, when you want to break its laws. Everything has to be sacrificed to your vanity—the country, Bertie, the children, your mother, me, the Throne, everything and everyone, so that you can be happy in your private life. You are mesmerized by your own legend.

QUEEN

Elizabeth, David is still the King.

DAVID

Don't forget you have a legend, too. The perfect wife and mother. I hope it's not making you smug.

BERTIE

David! You are not to be rude to Elizabeth! Do you hear? I won't have it! I will take over if necessary. But, David, let me put it to you this way—don't you think it's your duty to stay as king? You would do it better than anyone—no, he would, dear—don't you think it's your duty to stay even without Mrs. Simpson?

DAVID

It's my duty to try and be a good king . . . without her I'd be a bad one. So without her I cannot be king. I know it's unthinkable, but if Elizabeth were to leave you, do you think that you'd be a good king?

BERTIE

I'd try to be.

QUEEN

And you'd succeed, Bertie.

DAVID

Very possibly, Mamma. But you see, I'd fail. That's the difference between your sons. Without the woman I love beside me, I'd fail. (*They all look at him.*) So what can I do?

CURTAIN

SCENE THREE

AT RISE OF CURTAIN: *It is early evening two days later.*
MARGARET *comes in quickly.* MABELL *is sitting at desk
up left.*)

MARGARET

Mabell!

MABELL

Yes?

MARGARET

Have you heard the news? It's just been on the wireless.
It's over.

MABELL

What's over?

MARGARET

The crisis.

MABELL

He's abdicated.

MARGARET

No, no. She has.

103

MABELL

She can't. She's not queen.

MARGARET

No, no. She's given him up. She's issued a statement from the South of France saying she's withdrawing from an intolerable situation. So it's over. Aren't you delighted?

MABELL

No. Because it isn't over at all. It can't be. It's far, far too late.

MARGARET

But he hasn't abdicated yet.

MABELL

Morally he has.

MARGARET

Nothing's signed.

MABELL

He's committed to her beyond hope of recall. A month ago—even a week ago—a dignified joint statement renouncing each other and marriage could have worked, but now, after everything that's happened, how can he accept her renunciation?

MARGARET

But what if she insists?

MABELL

She can't. It would be pointless. She's his strength. He could only fight it out with her beside him and to force her renunciation she has to be beside him, too. The crisis can only end when he goes.

MARGARET

Goes?

MABELL

I'm sure of it.

MARGARET

You mean—goes—

MABELL

Yes. That's what I mean.

MARGARET

But everyone is begging him to stay.

MABELL

Yes, but none of them mean it, least of all the politicians. He interferes too much. Look at that visit to the Welsh miners. "Something must be done," he says. Well, *of course* something must be done, but even Attlee agrees the King can't tell the government in public what to do.

(PAGE *opens door up center. The* QUEEN *enters.*)

QUEEN

Well! This is a pretty kettle of fish. I've just heard the news from dear Archbishop Lang. What are we going to do now?

MARGARET

I hoped you were going to rest, ma'am.

QUEEN

So did I, Margaret dear, but some idiot from the Earl Marshal's office sent me fifty pages of foolscap about the forthcoming coronation. Quite apart from anything else, I would like to know whose coronation are they planning? David's or Bertie's? David was to abdicate today. Now he may not, only I don't know if David's king or if Bertie's king or even if we have a king at all. I've had just about as much as I can bear. (*She is very near tears.*)

(BERTIE *comes in up center.*)

BERTIE

Mamma, it's all over. I'm—King.

QUEEN

Oh, my dear boy. (MARGARET *and* MABELL *hastily withdraw up center, and such is their agitation that for once neither curtsies. The new King and his mother do not even notice that they have left.*)

BERTIE

I'd sooner face a firing squad than be k-king. I never wanted to be k-king. I can't even say the word.

QUEEN

Listen to me, Bertie.

BERTIE

It's the most terrible event in history, my becoming k—

QUEEN

Just listen to me. David was confident of success. Sure of it. Yet he failed.

BERTIE

I know, I know, and—and—

QUEEN

And unlike him, you'll succeed.

BERTIE

M—m—

QUEEN

Don't interrupt me. It was because he lacked your qualities that he failed.

BERTIE

He's clever. He's astute. He can talk to people. He can dominate a crowd. I've seen him. I can barely make a speech—if I have any popularity at all it's because of Elizabeth and the children.

QUEEN

You're like Papa. Very like Papa. He too had difficulties to overcome. You mustn't imagine that just because we were so popular at the end of our reign we were as popular at the beginning. Far from it. I hadn't Queen Alexandra's beauty. I hadn't her charm. Elizabeth is popular, but so are you. They know she would never have married a man not worthy of her.

BERTIE

You're saying all this to comfort me. But you're wrong. It'll all blow up in our faces.

QUEEN

What will?

BERTIE

The m—monarchy.

QUEEN

Nonsense.

BERTIE

I've had my first red boxes.

QUEEN

They are rather alarming.

BERTIE

I'd barely been king a minute when they were there

piled up in front of me. They've not been looked at for days. So I had to deal with them at once. (*He looks at his mother.*) I didn't know anything. It was the most terrible moment. T-Tommy Lascelles had to explain the simplest things to me. I've always been devoted to David all my life, supported him as best I could when he quarreled with Papa. I've never criticized him. Never. All right, he can't live without her. But surely he must have realized he was landing the rest of us in the most dreadful muddle.

QUEEN

I doubt it. And that is the difference between you. You would have thought of everyone else. Prepared them in good time. And that is why you will be a far better king than David would ever have been. Truly.

BERTIE

I c-can't speak. I could hardly get through the Accession address. I live in terror of the c-c- Oh, God! (*Pause, gets the words out slowly.*) Of . . . the . . . coronation . . . oath. You feel so bloody stupid standing there stammering. (*His panic at his own responsibility, the fact that his wife is ill, his fear of the future and his fury with his brother all combine to flood over him in his last moment of weakness. The* QUEEN *pats his head gently, breaks from him, walks about in agitation and then pulls herself together.*)

QUEEN

Yes. Well. The first thing for you to do is to have some whisky. (*She pours out a large glass of neat whisky.*)

I'm not quite sure what a double or a treble is, but I'm convinced this is a quadruple.

BERTIE (*taking it*)
It's enormous, Mamma. I shall be drunk.

QUEEN
Good.

BERTIE (*smiling*)
There's a crowd outside. I can't be seen leaving here in a state of intoxication.

QUEEN
I don't suppose, after the amazing events of the past week, it would in any way surprise them. All I do ask of you, Bertie, is not to fall flat on your face as you get into the car. It would be a discouraging start to your reign, which I feel sure will be in every way a tremendous success. Now let us look at all your assets and yes, your defects. We'll get rid of the latter first. You are shy. So was I. So was Queen Victoria. You don't know anything about the working of the government. Nor did your grandfather, and he came to the throne older than you. You stammer. That is all but conquered. It's only because you are upset that it is rather stronger today. Your coronation oath can be learnt and rehearsed in advance. You feel stupid stammering, but your audience admires your courage. Now your assets. They are so many I hardly know where to begin.

BERTIE

Mamma! Really!

QUEEN

I do not exaggerate. You have courage. Not just phys-
ical courage. Moral courage—and that's far more important. You persevere. That's how you conquered your
stammer. By perseverance. You're as good a mixer as
David. Look at your years in the Navy. Your splendid
boys' camps. You know quite as much about industrial
affairs, or else why did your brothers call you the Fore-
man? You are patient. David isn't. You're considerate.
He's not that either. You have true humility.

BERTIE

I have got Elizabeth. And the girls. And you, Mamma.

QUEEN

And me. And the family. We must all behave as if
nothing was wrong, nothing had happened.

BERTIE

Well, we'll do our best.

QUEEN

It's the only thing anyone can ever do. Tell me, is the
K—is David really going to broadcast?

BERTIE

Yes. The g-g-government has decided that now he's

no longer king they can't stop him. They don't want to be accused of censoring him.

QUEEN

I think it's a pity.

BERTIE

Hm. Personally, I think it a wise decision. He feels very strongly about it and a public statement from him will make it clear he is abdicating by his own choice. The B.B.C. were going to announce him as Mr. Edward Windsor.

QUEEN

That's quite wrong.

BERTIE

Don't worry. I told them that. As the son of a king he's a Royal Highness, so he'll be announced as Prince Edward. The Privy Council queried this, but I pointed out that if he's not royal he's a private citizen, and as such he could, if he wished, stand for Parliament. As that's the last thing anyone wants, they agreed with me at once. I shall give him a dukedom.

QUEEN

That would be best.

BERTIE

I'll suggest making him Duke of Windsor.

QUEEN

No—he can't take that title—it's the name of our dynasty.

BERTIE

Exactly. In time it will merge in with the rest of us. He's broadcasting from Windsor Castle after dinner tonight. I'm giving a family dinner for him at Royal Lodge.

QUEEN

I take it Elizabeth won't be there?

BERTIE

Apart from every other consideration, she's too ill. Her temperature's 103. But I hope you'll come.

QUEEN

Oh, yes. And after the broadcast?

BERTIE

He'll drive to Portsmouth. I've arranged for an unescorted destroyer to take him to France.

QUEEN

He said something about going to Switzerland.

BERTIE

He's changed his mind. Mrs. Simpson has arranged for him to stay with the Rothschilds in Vienna.

QUEEN

Poor David. What will his life be like now? And what's so awful for him is that he won't be able to marry Mrs. Simpson or even see her for six months. He's going to be very lonely.

BERTIE

Yes. (*There is a tiny silence.*)

QUEEN

You must go back to Elizabeth. Dear Bertie. (*She extends her hands to him. He kisses them and then embraces her warmly. He turns and goes to the door up center.*) Bertie. (*He turns. She curtsies to him. He bows and exits.*)

(*A moment later* MABELL *comes in up center.*)

QUEEN

Order a car for me, dear. I'm dining at Royal Lodge.

MABELL

That's better, ma'am.

QUEEN

What's better, dear?

MABELL

You look cheerful again.

Act Two

When I first curtsied to David he protested, looked embarrassed. I've just made my first curtsy to Bertie, to King George VI, and do you know, he accepted it as his right. He will make a good king.

CURTAIN

With the curtain down the Abdication Broadcast is heard over the front of house speakers.

BROADCAST

ANNOUNCER

This is Windsor Castle. His Royal Highness Prince Edward.

DUKE OF WINDSOR [DAVID]

At long last I am able to say a few words of my own. A few hours ago I discharged my last duty as King and Emperor and now that I have been succeeded by my brother, the Duke of York, my first words must be to declare my allegiance to him. This I do with all my heart.

You all know the reasons which have impelled me to renounce the Throne. But you must believe me when I tell you that I have found it impossible to carry the heavy burden of responsibility and to discharge my duties as King as I would wish to do without the help and support of the woman I love.

This decision has been made less difficult to me by the sure knowledge that my brother, with his long training in the public affairs of this country and with his fine qualities, will be able to take my place forthwith without interruption or injury to the life and progress of the Empire; and he has one matchless blessing enjoyed by so many of you and not bestowed on me—a happy home with his wife and children.

During these hard days I have been comforted by Her Majesty, my mother, and by her—by my family. Ministers of the Crown, and in particular Mr. Baldwin, the Prime Minister, have always treated me with full consideration.

I now quit altogether public affairs and I lay down my burden. It may be some time before I return to my native land, but I shall always follow the fortunes of the British race and Empire with profound interest, and if at any time in the future I can be found of service to His Majesty in a private station I shall not fail. And now we all have a new King. I wish him, and you, his people, happiness and prosperity with all my heart.

God bless you all.

God save the King.

SCENE FOUR

AT RISE OF CURTAIN: *It is afternoon nine years later in 1945.* DAVID *comes in, followed by* MARGARET.)

DAVID

I'm afraid I'm earlier than expected.

MARGARET

Her Majesty will be back in a moment, sir.

DAVID

Thank you.

MARGARET

The King and Queen had to cancel a drive through the East End, so Her Majesty went instead. I expect the crowds detained her.

DAVID

I expect so. How have you been keeping, Miss Wyndham?

117

MARGARET

Very well, thank you, sir. Of course we've all been working so hard for victory, we're all a bit tired, I think.

DAVID

And the Queen?

MARGARET

Very well, really. Like the rest of us, thankful the war is over. And you, sir? How are you?

DAVID

I'm quite well, too. (*There is a long pause.*) So is my wife.

MARGARET (*in an expressionless voice*)

I'm so glad. The Queen is really taking longer than I thought. The enthusiasm with which the royal family is greeted everywhere is remarkable.

DAVID

I'm sure. My brother and sister-in-law were always very popular.

MARGARET

Would you like tea now?

DAVID

No, no.

Act Two

MARGARET

I'm sure Her Majesty wouldn't want you to wait.

DAVID

I would prefer to, all the same. (*He smiles charmingly.*)
I'm so looking forward to seeing my family again. Of
course the Gloucesters are in Australia, but everyone
else is here. I shall stay at Harewood with my sister for
a while, too. And then there are all my old friends.
Monckton. Beaverbrook. Churchill.

MARGARET

I was shocked beyond measure when he lost the election.

DAVID

Were you? I wasn't.

MARGARET

He was so popular.

DAVID

Oh, but you can't rely on popularity.

MARGARET

No.

DAVID

Or on gratitude. Both are very ephemeral emotions.
Don't you agree?

MARGARET

Yes.

DAVID

No one votes out of gratitude. Tell me, is it true that no one dresses for dinner any more?

MARGARET

Oh, dear me no, sir. That's quite out.

DAVID

Amazing. Just as well my father wasn't alive to see that. I remember how cross he was when I took to wearing a bowler in London instead of a top hat. And there was very nearly a diplomatic incident when an American ambassador refused to wear knee breeches when he was being presented to my mother.

MARGARET

Times have changed, sir, as you wanted them to. No one wears court dress at all.

(*Enter* PAGE *up center.*)

PAGE

I thought you'd like to know, sir, the Queen's car is driving up.

DAVID

Oh. Thank you. John, isn't it?

Act Two

PAGE

PAGE

Yes, sir.

DAVID

That's not bad for nine years, is it?

PAGE

Marvelous, sir.

DAVID

Miss Wyndham, would you make sure my mother knows I'm here? (MARGARET *withdraws up center.*) John, is my mother very changed?

PAGE

No, sir. She uses a stick sometimes now, sir.

DAVID

A stick? I didn't know.

PAGE

That's the only difference really, sir. She liked living at Badminton. She loved going into the village and made great friends with the locals.

DAVID

Really! How splendid. Thank you, John.

(PAGE *goes to door, sees* QUEEN *approaching and opens*

both doors. The QUEEN *comes in. She is older, dressed in a coat and her famous toque, with a stick.* PAGE *withdraws.*)

QUEEN

My dear, dear boy.

DAVID

Mamma. (*They embrace. Pause.*)

QUEEN

How nice to see you. I was so sorry I was out. Bertie has a cold and then Elizabeth had to receive General de Gaulle, so I went to the East End for them.

DAVID

I was early. You look A-1, Mamma.

QUEEN

I'm older—older. Well—well—well. Sit down, David. I'm so delighted to see you again. So much has happened. (*They sit. There is an awkward pause.*)

DAVID

London doesn't seem so very changed. I thought the damage would be worse.

QUEEN

I've only just moved back here. This room and my bedroom arc all right. There's a great deal to do elsewhere. Everywhere, in fact. Was Paris badly bombed?

DAVID

Not really. (*A pause.*)

QUEEN

You're very brown, David. It suits you.

DAVID

Five years in the Bahamas.

QUEEN

Yes, of course. There's a great deal of clearing up to do in the world, so we'll all be very busy. All my treasures to be got out of store. They were sent somewhere in Wales. I suppose you had to leave everything behind when you escaped to Spain? (DAVID *deliberately seizes his chance and firmly mentions his wife.*)

DAVID

Wallis and I have been very lucky and most of our things haven't been damaged or looted.

QUEEN (*avoiding the challenge*)

Didn't you write and say there were land mines in your garden?

DAVID

In the south of France at La Croe. Not in Paris.

QUEEN

Are they cleared away yet?

DAVID

Not yet. We can't live at La Croe until they are. We were wondering what to do. Our lease is up in 1947.

QUEEN

You could renew it, I suppose. It might be wise. (*The hint is not taken.*)

DAVID

Living in France was only a temporary measure. We're not certain we want to stay there. (*The "we" is faintly emphasized.*)

QUEEN (*easily*)

I'll ring for tea. We're still rationed. I'm told we will be for some time. I hope these bells are working. They weren't, but someone at last came and put them right. (*She rises.*) You're dining with Bertie and Elizabeth tonight?

DAVID

Yes.

QUEEN

I must prepare you, I think. He's older. He's very tired. You'll find he looks it.

DAVID

I'm sure.

QUEEN

He never spared himself throughout the war. Nor did
she. I think they worked harder than anyone else in
the country. I really do. They're very, very popular.

DAVID

I was sure they would be. I am so glad, Mamma.

QUEEN

I was reading the Parliamentary reports yesterday.
The Colonial Secretary was very complimentary about
your administration in the Bahamas. I was delighted.
I was so proud of you. (*The* QUEEN *is striving to be
warm and friendly.*)

DAVID

Wallis worked tremendously hard to help me. Any
success I had is as much hers as mine.

QUEEN

Marina hopes you'll go and see her at Coppins.

DAVID

How is she?

QUEEN

I think she's recovering at last from Georgie's death.
Her grief was overwhelming. I miss him.

DAVID

So do I.

QUEEN

Eventually I had to tell her that in the family we cannot have the luxury of a private grief. Or of private joys, for that matter.

(PAGE *enters up center.*)

QUEEN

Oh, good! The bell is working.

PAGE

Yes, ma'am.

QUEEN

Tea, please. (PAGE *bows and exits.*)

DAVID

Nothing has changed, Mamma.

QUEEN

Certain values never change, no matter what happens. I believe we're going to have a welfare state. A revolution without the upheaval of one. I don't quite understand it all. Mr. Attlee is very persuasive on the subject. I like him.

DAVID
I thought I'd go and look at the Fort.

QUEEN
It must be terribly overgrown. Why distress yourself needlessly?

DAVID
Wallis and I thought—if we weren't going to get another job—another governorship—we might settle there again.

QUEEN (*accepting the challenge this time*)
That would be a mistake.

DAVID
Wallis and I have been happily married for eight years. Does that mean nothing to you?

QUEEN
To know that you are happy means a great deal to me. But it doesn't alter the basic principle. Neither Elizabeth nor I can receive anyone who is divorced. She is the wife of the Head of the Church and I am his mother. As to the question of a job, what job? You refused Bermuda.

DAVID
Whose macabre idea was that? I cannot agree to being

127

shunted from remote island to remote island. It's a wonder I wasn't offered St. Helena.

QUEEN

Bermuda would have accepted you. Nowhere else will. You do not seem to understand at all how very upset the entire Empire was at your abdication. No self-governing dominion will accept you. Bertie cannot force you upon any of the colonies, since it is obvious you will take your wife with you. It means he would be suggesting as the Governor's consort a woman his wife and mother cannot receive.

DAVID

Wallis has done more work as the Governor's wife than any other Governor's wife. Did you know that she ran canteens, organized clinics? Any other woman would have received a decoration. She has received nothing, not even a letter of thanks. As the wife of a retiring Governor she's entitled to be received at Buckingham Palace. Because she's my wife she isn't.

QUEEN

Not because she's your wife. Because she's divorced.

DAVID

It must be lovely for you and Elizabeth to feel that you've never even made two mistakes. You base your views on Christian morals, but what is Christian about them? Christ forgave people. You don't.

Act Two

Dear David, we are meeting after nearly nine years.
Please, please do not let us quarrel now. (*Quickly.*)
The reason for our separation grieves me beyond be-
lief, but I couldn't change then and I can't change
now. Let us accept the position. With mutual good
will and tolerance it should be possible for us to meet
without these upsets.

DAVID

Mutual good will? I've been full of good will for you
all ever since I abdicated. But there's no return of
good will to me or to my wife. Why did Bertie
deny Wallis her true position as my wife? Why is she
not acknowledged a Royal Highness?

QUEEN

The government advised against it.

DAVID

Yes, of course. They all hated me. Very convenient.

QUEEN

The Dominion governments advised against it. You
had abdicated.

DAVID

I am a Royal Highness by right of birth. Bertie did
not make me one and he knew it. My marriage is legal,

129

consequently according to the laws of this country, my wife must take my position. If I'm king she is queen. If I'm a prince she is a princess.

QUEEN

As monarch, Bertie has to act within the wishes of the government.

DAVID

Not even a government can act illegally, and Bertie's action in barring Wallis from her full position as my wife is illegal. I could fight a lawsuit—I am advised I have an excellent case. I could have refused to sell Bertie Balmoral and Sandringham just as I could settle in England in defiance of your wishes and the British public be subjected to the edifying spectacle of lawsuits within the royal family. Oh, don't worry, I won't. But when you are reflecting, as I'm sure you often do, on the innumerable virtues of your second son and his wife, you might just occasionally remember that your first son and his wife are not without virtue either.

(PAGE *enters up center with tea trolley.*)

QUEEN

Is the lift working?

PAGE

It's a bit hesitant still, ma'am.

QUEEN

Put the trolley by me. Thank you, John. David, will
you bring up that table. (PAGE *exits.*) There's bread
and butter. I don't quite know what this cake is made
of.

DAVID

Thank you.

QUEEN

Will you be staying in London long?

DAVID

Only a week or so. We have to get our things in order
in Paris. Wallis is very busy. There's a lot to do.

QUEEN

Of course. (*She pauses.*) You must both be busy.
(DAVID *glances at her. She pours tea.*)

DAVID

Like you, we've been living out of suitcases in other
people's houses. We can't wait to get into our own
home. Of course our Paris house, like La Croe, is only
rented, but there's a house not far from it we want
to buy.

QUEEN (*casually*)
Are Paris houses very expensive?

DAVID

No more so than in London, I should imagine. I haven't gone into it yet. It'll be very convenient living in Paris, though. I can pop over and see you from time to time.

QUEEN

I'd like that, David, so much.

(PAGE *enters up center.*)

PAGE

A telephone call for His Royal Highness.

DAVID

Who is it?

PAGE

It's from Paris, sir. (*Exit.*)

DAVID

That'll be Wallis. If you'll excuse me, Mamma—

QUEEN

Of course. (*He starts to go.*) Oh, David.

DAVID

Mamma?

QUEEN

I send a kind message to your wife.

DAVID

Thank you, Mamma. That's very good of you. (DAVID *exits. The* QUEEN, *seated bolt upright as always, pours herself another cup of tea. She has unbent as far as she is able. As she calmly sips her tea:*)

THE CURTAIN FALLS